CLOUDS IN SPACE

CLOUDS IN SPACE

Nebulae, Stardust, and Us

TERESA ROBESON

illustrated by DIĀNA RENŽINA

≡ mit Kids Press

WANT TO KNOW A SECRET?

When you look up after sunset
—to count the stars,
glimpse a glancing meteor,
or marvel at the moon—

there are things you can't clearly see
suspended in the cosmos
beyond the dark curtain of night.

WHAT'S OUT THERE?
It's . . .

Long ago,
when telescopes were first invented,
people could only see
me and my nebula friends
as fuzzy smudges in the sky.

So they thought
I was a faraway cloud.

Sure, clouds and I *are* similar,
like third cousins are similar.

Clouds float
          and I float.
Clouds contain dust;
          I am dusty, too.

Clouds can look like all
kinds of things:

a bunny,

a turtle,

a mouse.

Same here! I can look like a **BUTTERFLY,**

an **ELEPHANT,**

and, yes,

a TURTLE!

BUT . . .

we are also different.

While clouds can be large,
spanning hundreds of miles
across the sky,

I am immense,

S-T-R-E-T-C-H-I-N-G

thousands of miles,
light-years in width.

While clouds appear white
and many shades of gray,

I am a kaleidoscope,
a riot of rainbows,
atoms aglow with starlight.

To reach a cloud,
hop on a plane and soar up, up, up.

Or wait for a foggy morning,
and a cloud will drift down to you.

But to visit me,
you'll need a spaceship of great speed.

Even flying as fast as a beam of light,
it will take seven hundred years or more!

While clouds can provide shade
or give you rain,

I provided all the parts
to give you . . .
             YOU!

HOW?

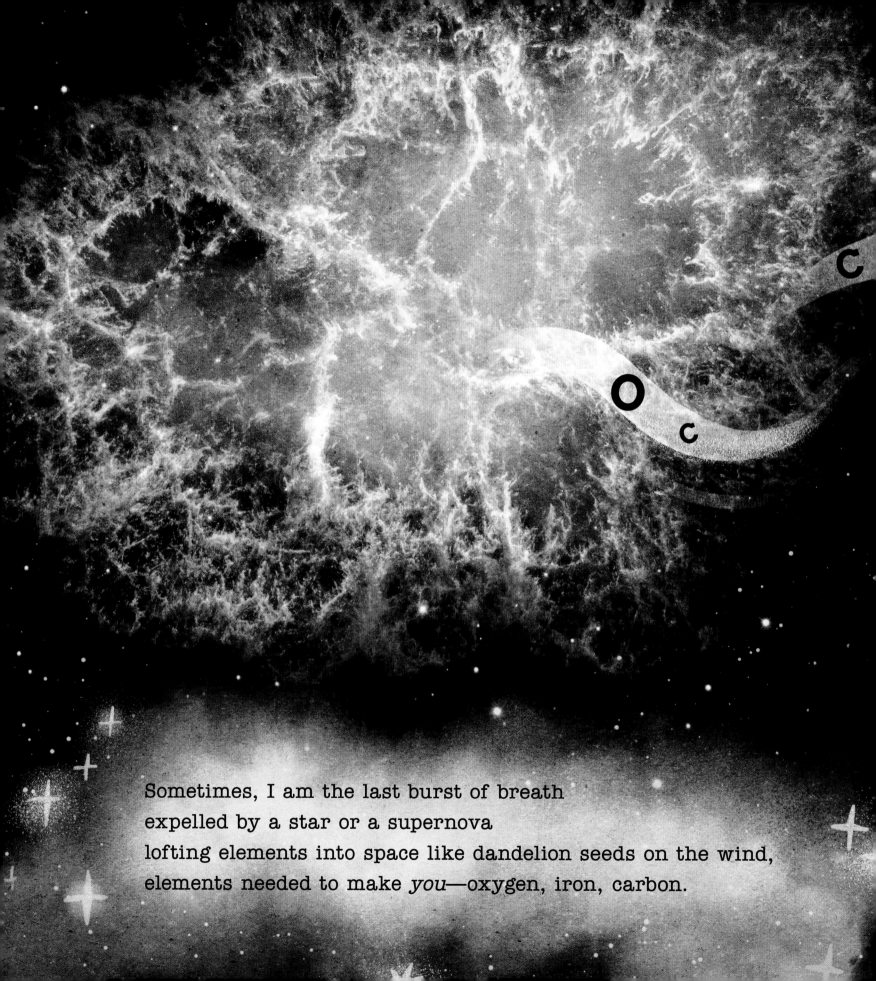

Sometimes, I am the last burst of breath
expelled by a star or a supernova
lofting elements into space like dandelion seeds on the wind,
elements needed to make *you*—oxygen, iron, carbon.

Other times, I am a stellar nursery,
pulling together molecules
from those last gasps of supernovae,
swirling and twirling them . . .

to create stars, planets,

your world, and, of course . . .

YOU.

You are grown from scattered stardust,
sprouted in a stellar nursery.

**I AM THE STARDUST
AND THE NURSERY.**

We are family forged in fire,
separated by space and time.

PLEIADES

And that is the secret:
me and you,
and clouds, too,
we're all connected
in this grand universe.

So after sunset, when you look up
    —to count the stars,
    glimpse a glancing meteor,
    or marvel at the moon—

whisper my name,

NEBULA.

I'll be waving back.

THE DISCOVERY OF NEBULAE

Astronomy, the study of everything that's outside our planet, is considered the first science. Before people even had a word for science, they looked up at the sky. They noticed how the sun moved and when and where the moon appeared. They observed how the stars seemed to be grouped into shapes and how those shapes moved together as the seasons changed. Eventually, when humans began studying the world around them in a systematic way, astronomy became its own branch of science.

Around the early seventeenth century, when telescopes were invented, people peering through them saw hazy patches that looked like space clouds, which they called "nebulae." In fact, they called all the fuzzy things they saw in the sky nebulae. It wasn't until much later, in the twentieth century, when larger, more sophisticated telescopes were invented, that astronomers realized some of the fuzzy patches were really galaxies and star clusters, while others were true nebulae made of dust and gases.

Most nebulae are so far away that we need special equipment to see them from Earth. The few that we can see with the naked eye look like starry dots (such as the Orion Nebula) or faint patches of light (such as the Lagoon Nebula).

HOW NEBULAE FORM

Unlike clouds, which form on Earth when the sun's heat causes moisture to evaporate and then condense, nebulae are found only in space. There are three different ways nebulae can form, and two involve dying stars flinging out materials.

At the end of their lives, medium-size stars like our sun puff up and "exhale" gas and dust like a smoke ring. This breath of gas and dust becomes a nebula.

Other, bigger stars also expand before dying. But they are so massive and push out with such force that they explode. Exploding stars are called supernovae, and their explosions create nebulae of dust and gases.

The third way nebulae form is the opposite of the other two. Instead of stars tossing out gases and dust, gravitational forces pull particles together, forming bigger and bigger clumps. It's sort of like a party getting more and more crowded as everyone invites more friends.

TYPES OF NEBULAE

Scientists have classified nebulae into two main categories: dark and bright.

Dark nebulae have no nearby stars to reflect light from or heat them up. They're cold clumps of gas and dust that act like a black curtain, blocking the light of stars behind them from ever reaching us and creating a dark patch in the sky.

Bright nebulae come in two varieties: reflection and emission. Reflection nebulae shine by bouncing off light from nearby stars, just like our moon does. Emission nebulae glow with the heat of nearby stars.

Planetary nebulae are a special kind of emission nebula that form from dying and exploding stars. They don't actually have to do with planets! They got their name because people once mistakenly thought planetary nebulae were stars with planets forming around them, since telescopes weren't strong enough to make out what they were.

As more powerful telescopes are built, new nebulae are being discovered. Space is a really, really, really big place after all, and there's a lot of sky left to explore. If you become an astronomer, maybe you'll discover and name a nebula! Turn the page to revisit the ones you've seen in this book—and see a few new ones!

CAST

(In Order of Appearance)

The locations for the nebulae are constellations.

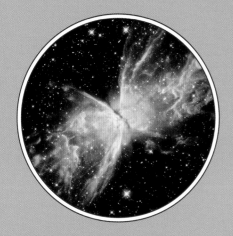

◀ **BUTTERFLY NEBULA**

planetary nebula in Scorpius

ELEPHANT TRUNK NEBULA ▶

emission nebula in Cepheus

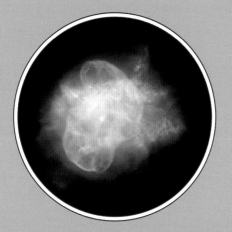

◀ **TURTLE NEBULA**

planetary nebula in Hercules

TARANTULA NEBULA ▶

emission nebula in Dorado

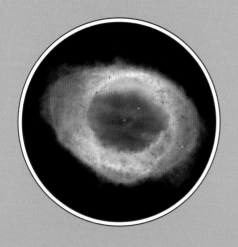

◀ **RING NEBULA**

planetary nebula in Lyra

HELIX NEBULA ▶
planetary nebula in Aquarius

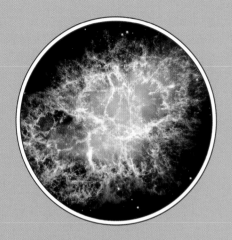

◀ **CRAB NEBULA**
planetary nebula in Taurus

OTHER STAR-STUDDED NEBULAE

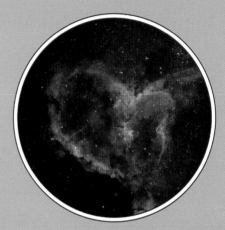

HEART NEBULA ▶
emission nebula in Cassiopeia

◀ **ANT NEBULA**
planetary nebula in Norma

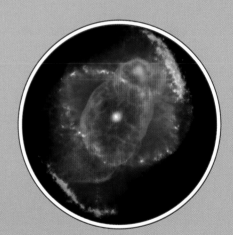

CAT'S EYE NEBULA ▶
planetary nebula in Draco

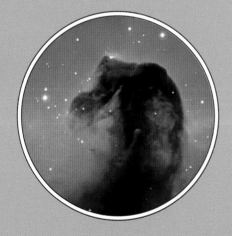

◀ **HORSEHEAD NEBULA**
dark nebula in Orion

WEBSITES TO EXPLORE

NASA Kids' Club–for elementary school students:

https://www.nasa.gov/kidsclub/index.html

Science News Explores–for middle and high school students:

https://www.snexplores.org/topic/space

BIBLIOGRAPHY

Bakich, Michael E. *The Complete Star Atlas: A Practical Guide to Viewing the Night Sky.* Waukesha, WI: Kalmbach Media, 2020.

Bell, Jim. *Hubble Legacy: 30 Years of Discoveries and Images.* New York: Sterling Publishing, 2020.

Eicher, David J., and Brian May, creative director. *Cosmic Clouds 3-D: Where Stars Are Born.* Cambridge, MA: The MIT Press, 2020.

Harwood, William. *Space Odyssey: Voyaging through the Cosmos.* Washington, DC: National Geographic Society, 2001.

Moore, Patrick, ed. *Astronomy Encyclopedia.* New York: Oxford University Press, 2002.

Scagell, Robin. *Children's Night Sky Atlas: The Essential Skywatching Guide Complete with Detailed Maps, Stunning Photography, and See-Through Pages.* New York: DK Publishing, 2004.

TERESA ROBESON is the APALA Picture Book Award–winning author of *Queen of Physics: How Wu Chien Shiung Helped Unlock the Secrets of the Atom* and *Two Bicycles in Beijing.* She lives on twenty-seven acres in southern Indiana, where she relaxes by birding, keeping up with science, making soap, knitting, baking, and trying to impress the chickens with her bilingualism.

DIĀNA RENŽINA studied design and worked at several creative agencies before becoming a full-time illustrator and digital designer. Her work is often inspired by Latvian mythology and nature, and when she's not drawing, she enjoys photography, dancing the tango, and exploring the outdoors. She lives in Riga, Latvia, a city of cobbled streets, pine forests, Art Nouveau architecture, and the cold sea.

This book would not exist without Peter Vogel, my high school physics
and computer science teacher, who encouraged my love of astronomy;
Tracy Marchini, my agent, who found the absolute perfect publisher;
and Olivia Swomley at Candlewick, whose warm enthusiasm
shone like a supernova. My immense gratitude to them all!
TR

To Ronis and Marusja, best team ever
DR

Text copyright © 2024 by Teresa Robeson
Illustrations copyright © 2024 by Diāna Renžina
CREDITS FOR PHOTOS USED WITHIN ILLUSTRATIONS: Butterfly nebula: NASA, ESA, and J. Kastner (RIT). Elephant trunk nebula: T.A. Rector (University of Alaska Anchorage) and WIYN/NOIRLab/NSF/AURA. Turtle nebula: ESA/Hubble and NASA. Tarantula nebula: NASA and ESA. Ring nebula: NASA, ESA, and the Hubble Heritage (STScI/AURA)-ESA/Hubble Collaboration. Helix nebula: NASA, ESA, C.R. O'Dell (Vanderbilt University), and M. Meixner, P. McCullough, and G. Bacon (Space Telescope Science Institute). Crab nebula: NASA, ESA, and J. Hester and A. Loll (Arizona State University). Heart nebula: ESA/Hubble and NASA. Ant nebula: NASA, ESA, and the Hubble Heritage Team (STScI/AURA); Acknowledgment: R. Sahai (Jet Propulsion Lab) and B. Balick (University of Washington). Cat's eye nebula: J.P. Harrington and K.J. Borkowski (University of Maryland) and NASA–HST's Greatest Hits. Horsehead nebula: Ken Crawford.

Cover illustrations copyright © 2024 by Diāna Renžina
Butterfly nebula photo courtesy of NASA, ESA, and J. Kastner (RIT)
Turtle nebula photo courtesy of ESA/Hubble and NASA

The MIT Press, the ☰mit Kids Press colophon, and MIT Kids Press are trademarks of The MIT Press,
a department of the Massachusetts Institute of Technology, and used under license from The MIT Press.
The colophon and MIT Kids Press are registered in the US Patent and Trademark Office.

First edition 2024

Library of Congress Catalog Card Number 2023943712
ISBN 978-1-5362-2537-2

24 25 26 27 28 29 CCP 10 9 8 7 6 5 4 3 2 1

Printed in Shenzhen, Guangdong, China

This book was typeset in ITC American Typewriter and Arvo.
The illustrations were created digitally.

MIT Kids Press
an imprint of Candlewick Press
99 Dover Street
Somerville, Massachusetts 02144

mitkidspress.com
candlewick.com